D0722776

Structural Wonders

Statue of Liberty

Jennifer Hurtig

Published by Weigl Publishers Inc.
350 5th Avenue, Suite 3304, PMB 6G
New York, NY 10118-0069

Website: www.weigl.com

Library of Congress Cataloging-in-Publication Data

Hurtig, Jennifer.
The Statue of Liberty/ Jennifer Hurtig.
    p. cm.—(Structural wonders)
Includes index.
ISBN 978-1-59036-940-1 (hard cover: alk. Paper) –
ISBN 978-1-59036-941-8 (soft cover: alk. Paper) etc.—Juvenile literature. I. Title
F128.64.L6H87 2009
9747'1—dc22

2008015665

Printed in the United States of America
1 2 3 4 5 6 7 8 9 0 12 11 10 09 08

Photograph Credits
Weigl acknowledges Getty Images as its primary image supplier.

Project Coordinators: Heather C. Hudak, Heather Kissock
Design: Terry Paulhus

Contents

What is the Statue of Liberty?

The Statue of Liberty is one of the planet's best-known monuments. Also known as Liberty Enlightening the World, it stands as a symbol of the United States of America. It marks the principles of **democracy** and freedom on which that country is based. The statue represents liberty and escape from **oppression**.

Located in the New York harbor, the Statue of Liberty was one of the first **landmarks** immigrants to the United States saw when they arrived by ship. To many of these people, the statue symbolized what they hoped to find in America—freedom and acceptance. The sight of the Statue of Liberty gave them hope for a fresh start and a new future.

The Statue of Liberty was given to the United States by France in 1886. It was a gift for the centennial of America's Declaration of Independence. It also celebrated the friendship between the two nations. Both France and the United States share similar histories. They waged wars in the 1700s to become **republics** that were free from the rule of a **monarch**.

France was a key ally during the American Revolution. It supplied the United States with weapons, soldiers, and funds. France shared in the American victory and sought to copy the United States. Presenting the United States with a gift to mark its centennial seemed an appropriate way to show France's respect and admiration. It also was seen as a way of promoting France's current government. When the idea for this gift was created, many people in France wanted a return to the rule of a monarch. Politicians believed that giving this large gift to a fellow republic would encourage the people of France to remain a republic.

Quick Bites

- From 1886 to 1902, the Statue of Liberty was used as a lighthouse.
- The island on which the Statue of Liberty stands was once called Bedloe's Island. In 1956, it was renamed Liberty Island.
- The Statue of Liberty began to show signs of damage in the 1970s. It cost more than $230 million and took longer than two years to **restore** the statue.

History of the Statue

The idea to build a statue was first proposed in 1865 at a dinner party attended by French sculptor, Frédéric Auguste Bartholdi. During dinner, conversation turned to the United States and its success in building a democratic nation after years of British rule. Even though the centennial was 11 years away, the people at the dinner party felt that France should give a gift to the United States. They wanted to show their support for the country's leadership in promoting democracy around the world.

Bartholdi thought about the idea for a long time. By 1871, he had developed a concept for the statue. Bartholdi journeyed to New York to promote the idea to the United States. He also wanted to search for a site to place the statue. When he arrived by ship in the harbor of Bedloe's Island, Bartholdi knew that it was the perfect site for the Statue of Liberty.

Bartholdi's model of the statue is in Paris's Jardin du Luxembourg.

The United States accepted Bartholdi's proposal. They agreed that the statue would be built in France, and the base would be built in the United States. Upon returning to France, Bartholdi set to work on a model of the statue. The model was approved in 1875, and fund-raising began to get the money to build the statue. In 1877, the U.S. government officially declared Bedloe's Island as the location for the Statue of Liberty.

Twenty years passed from the first discussion of the statue to its completion in 1885.

1865: The plan to build a statue is hatched at a dinner party in France.

1875: Bartholdi's model is approved. Construction starts.

1877: The U.S. government designates Bedloe's Island as the future home of the statue.

1883: Construction begins on the pedestal, or base, of the statue.

1884: The statue is completed in France.

1885: The statue is shipped in pieces to the United States.

1886: The pedestal is completed in April. On October 28, the completed Statue of Liberty is dedicated.

1982: Plans for restoring of the Statue of Liberty are put into place.

1984: The restoration begins. The statue is designated as a **UNESCO World Heritage Site**.

July 5, 1986: The restoration of the Statue of Liberty is complete.

The Statue of Liberty's head was displayed in the Champs du Mars during the 1878 World's Fair in Paris.

Joseph Pulitzer, a journalist, helped raise the money to build the base of the statue.

Due to its massive size, the statue had special construction needs. Bartholdi hired Gustave Eiffel to design the framework for the statue so it would be sturdy. Gustave Eiffel was well-known for building metal structures, such as the Eiffel Tower in Paris, France. Eiffel hired out the detailed work to another engineer, Maurice Koechlin.

Due to problems with funding on both sides of the ocean, the statue was not completed in time for the centennial. In fact, it was shipped to New York in 1885, nine years late. The statue was so large that it had to be split into 350 pieces and packed in 214 crates for shipping. During its voyage, the ship almost sank because of the weight. The ship arrived in New York on June 17. Over the next year, the statue was reconstructed on its base. It was presented to the public on October 28, 1886. On this day, more than 20, 000 people viewed the statue.

The statue features a woman lifting a torch in her right hand. She is stepping out of the shackles that bind her. These elements help to show how the statue represents freedom.

Big Ideas

From its tip to its base, Bartholdi put much thought into the design of the Statue of Liberty. Almost every detail of the statue has symbolic meaning, leading to the idea of liberty enlightening the world.

At the top of the statue, a crown rests upon the woman's head. The crown has seven spikes. These spikes represent the seven seas and seven continents of the world. They represent the idea that people all over the world should have the right to freedom. The crown has 25 windows. Rays of sunlight reflect upward from the windows, symbolizing the way a person seems to glow when he or she has been enlightened.

Lady Liberty carries a tablet in her left hand. The tablet represents the law and principles on which the United States is founded. The date of America's independence, July 4, 1776, is written on the tablet.

Even the base of the statue is symbolic. It is made up of 13 layers of granite. These layers represent the 13 founding colonies of the United States. A poem to freedom is engraved on the statue's pedestal. Emma Lazarus wrote the poem to help raise funds for the pedestal.

Web Link:
To find out more about the symbolism of the Statue of Liberty, visit www.statueliberty.net.

1) The tablet is placed near Lady Liberty's heart. This may be to remind people of the importance of Independence Day. 2) The woman wears an ancient Roman style of clothing to represent the goddess "Libertas." This goddess was worshiped by people who had been freed from slavery. 3) Bartholdi's mother, Charlotte, is often believed to have been the model for the Statue of Liberty's face.

Profile:
Frédéric Auguste Bartholdi

Frédéric Auguste Bartholdi was born on August 2, 1834, in Colmar, a town in the French province of Alsace. It was in Alsace that he first began training to be an **architect**. Bartholdi later moved to Paris to study painting and sculpture. He is best-known for his work as a sculptor.

Bartholdi's first well-known statue was the General Rapp's monument in Colmar. Jean Rapp was a general under Napoleon Bonaparte, one of France's best-known leaders. Rapp was also a native of Colmar. Bartholdi's statue of General Rapp demonstrated what was to become his signature style—its large size. The statue was 12 feet (3.7 meters) tall. Bartholdi was only 18 years old when he made this statue.

A few years after creating this monument, Bartholdi traveled to Egypt and Yemen. There, he was inspired by the large size of the Pyramids and Sphinx at Giza. While in Egypt, Bartholdi met Count Ferdinand-Marie de Lesseps. The count was in the process of building the Suez Canal, a structure that would stretch from the Mediterranean to the Red Sea.

THE WORK OF FRÉDÉRIC AUGUSTE BARTHOLDI

Lion of Belfort
Considered Bartholdi's masterpiece, this statue is located in Belfort, France. The huge lion was carved into the side of a sandstone mountain in 1880. It was created to commemorate the struggle the French faced in holding off the Prussian forces during the Franco-Prussian War.

Switzerland Succoring Strasbourg
This statue was made as a gift from France to Switzerland to show France's appreciation for Switzerland's help in the Franco-Prussian War. Bartholdi created the statue in 1895. It can be seen in Basel, Switzerland, near the town's train station.

Bartholdi was impressed with the project and wanted to contribute to it by building a statue for the Suez Canal. The statue was never built, but it was planned to be a female in a robe, wearing a headband and holding a torch.

Instead, Bartholdi focused his attention on building a symbolic gift for the United States. This gift, the Statue of Liberty, raised Bartholdi's profile around the world. As a result, he was contracted to create more sculptures. In France, his work can be found in his hometown of Colmar, as well as in Paris, Lyon, and Belfort. After designing the Statue of Liberty, Bartholdi continued to receive contracts within the United States. He designed fountains, statues, and monuments for the cities of Boston, New York, and Washington, DC.

Frédéric Auguste Bartholdi died of tuberculosis on October 4, 1904, in Paris. At the time of his death, he was considered one of the world's greatest sculptors.

The Suez Canal opened in 1869. Plans for a statue at the Suez Canal instead were used for the Statue of Liberty.

Lafayette and Washington
This statue of Marquis de Lafayette and George Washington is bronze with a marble base. George Washington was a general during the American Revolution. He later became the United States' first president. Marquis de Lafayette was a French military leader who fought on behalf of the Americans during the American Revolution. Bartholdi completed the statue in Paris in 1895. It was then moved to its current location in New York City's Morningside Park.

Bartholdi Fountain
Bartholdi made the Bartholdi Fountain for the 1876 International Centennial Exhibition in Philadelphia. Following the exhibition, the United States government bought the fountain for $6,000. It was moved to Washington, DC, in 1877. Today, it sits in the United States Botanic Gardens.

The Science Behind the Building

While planning the construction of the Statue of Liberty, Bartholdi had to think about the outdoor environment in which it would be sitting. The statue would face many types of weather, ranging from high winds to rain to snow. The salty humidity of the ocean air also could damage the statue. Bartholdi had to use durable materials that would withstand the environment. For this reason, the main materials used to create the statue were iron, steel, copper, and granite.

The Properties of Iron

Iron is a versatile and strong material. With the use of heat, it easily can be molded into different shapes. Once it is set into a shape, iron stays firmly in position. It carries the weight of the other materials involved in the structure. This was very helpful when creating the framework inside the Statue of Liberty. The inner framework of the statue is made up of four iron posts that run from the bottom to the top of the statue. The posts form a pylon at the top to bear the weight of the statue. Smaller beams come from the central tower of iron. These beams support the statue's shell.

New York has hot summers and cold winters. Snow, heat, sleet, and rain are some of the weather conditions the Statue of Liberty must face.

The Properties of Copper

The shell, or outside, of the statue is made up of copper sheets that have been fastened to the frame. One of the main advantages of using copper on the outside of the statue is that it does not corrode, or rust, easily. This means that it can face all kinds of weather, including wind, rain, snow, and sunlight, without being degraded. Copper is easily molded. This allows workers to shape the sheets into the statue's parts.

The Properties of Granite

The Statue of Liberty sits on a pedestal that is made mainly of granite. Granite is known to be one of the strongest building stones on Earth. It is able to bear incredibly heavy loads. This strength made it an ideal material to use as a base for the statue. Granite is very weather-resistant. This means that it can withstand severe and varied weather conditions, such as those often found along the New York coast.

Web Link:
To find out more about about copper, go to www.copper.org.

Science and Technology

When Bartholdi first designed the Statue of Liberty, he made a model that was 4 feet (1.25 m) high. After taking very exact measurements of every part of his model, Bartholdi built another model. This model was 9 feet (2.85 m) tall. Once the second model was complete, he made another that was one-fourth of the height of the actual statue. After the finishing touches had been put on the quarter-scale model, it was cut into 300 pieces. Bartholdi and his workers made thousands of measurements of each piece, so that they could multiply the measurements by four to reach the final size of the statue. These accurate measurements made sure that the full-size statue would look just like the models Bartholdi had sculpted. To build the final statue, Bartholdi used many tools.

Many artists, architects, and engineers make scale models before building an actual structure or object.

Mallets

To create the outer shell of the statue, workers pounded thin sheets of copper onto each piece. They did this using tools called mallets. Mallet heads can be made out of many different materials. Some mallets are made from materials such as wood and rubber. They are used for working with soft metals, such as copper, because they do not leave dents or marks. Mallets are designed to swing faster and hit harder than human arms. This is a property of tools is called mechanical advantage. Mechanical advantage tools can accomplish more work with the same effort.

A mallet looks similar to a hammer, but often it has a larger head.

More than 300,000 rivets were used in building the Statue of Liberty.

Rivets

To connect all 300 sheets of copper that make up the outer layer of the statue, workers used metal connectors called rivets. Rivets look like stubby nails. They have a thick, blunt shaft, with a round head at one end. Rivets are very good at resisting a force called shear. Shear is the force that pulls **perpendicular** to the shaft of the rivet. In the Statue of Liberty, shear occurs when one heavy copper sheet pulls down on the sheet above it. The builders of the statue used many rivets, to make sure that each rivet would have less shear to deal with on its own. This meant that each single rivet would be less likely to break.

Cranes

Large cranes were used to move pieces of copper and iron for the Statue of Liberty. Cranes use pulley systems. Pulley systems are wheels that are wrapped in ropes or cables and are used to move a load. An object that needs to be moved is attached to one end of the rope or cable. The other end of the rope or cable is then pulled, and the object is lifted. The wheel changes the direction of force. This allows loads to be lifted to great heights by applying force to the rope at the ground level.

Quick Bites

While copper is a reddish-orange color, the Statue of Liberty is green. This has occurred as a result of the weather. Humidity, wind, and other forms of weather interact with the copper. Over time, this causes a coating, or patina, to appear. This green patina protects the copper from corrosion.

Computer-Aided Design

Architects are trained professionals who work with clients to design structures. Before anything is built, they make detailed drawings or models. These plans are important tools that help people visualize what the structure will look like. A blueprint is a detailed diagram that shows where all the parts of the structure will be placed. Walls, doors, windows, plumbing, electrical wiring, and other details are mapped out on the blueprint. Blueprints act as a guide for engineers and builders during construction.

For centuries, architects and builders worked without the aid of computers. Sketches and blueprints were drawn by hand. Highly skilled drafters would draw very technical designs. Today, this process is done using computers and sophisticated software programs. Architects use CAD, or computer-aided design, throughout the design process. Early CAD systems used computers to draft building plans. Today's computer programs can do much more. They can build three-dimensional models and computer simulations of how a building will look. They can also calculate the effects of different physical forces on the structure. Using CAD, today's architects can build more complex structures at lower cost and in less time.

Computer-aided design programs have been used since the 1960s.

Eye on Design

Preserving Design with 3-D Lasers

While the Statue of Liberty was built using materials that ensured long-term durability, there is no guarantee that the materials will last forever. The statue has already needed one restoration to repair damage. Over time, entire pieces of the statue may need to be replaced.

Traditional methods of measuring, such as using a tape measure, do not provide the detail needed to rebuild parts the Statue of Liberty.

There is very little information about the original construction of the statue. A fire in the factory where the statue was made destroyed many of the original drawings, as well as all of the molds used to create each piece of the statue. Until recently, a reconstruction of the statue would have required guesswork. Now, with the use of 3-D laser technology, scientists have been able to record the specifications of the Statue of Liberty.

Researchers used a 3-D laser instrument to scan the Statue of Liberty and record measurements of its pieces. The information was received in the form of laser pulses. This data was turned into a digital model of the statue. Measurements from the model can used to rebuild parts of the statue that become damaged.

MEASURING THE STATUE OF LIBERTY

Location

The Statue of Liberty is located on Liberty Island in New York.

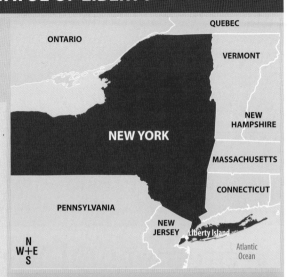

Height

- The total height of the Statue of Liberty from the ground to the torch is 305 feet and 1 inch (92.99 m).
- The statue measures 151 feet and 1 inch (46.05 m) from the top of the base to the top of the torch.

Weight

The weight of the Statue of Liberty is 450,000 pounds (204,117 kilograms). The metal used in the statue weighs a total of 312,000 pounds (141,521 kg). The concrete **foundation** of the statue weighs 54 million pounds (24,493,988 kg).

Other Interesting Facts

- The face of the Statue of liberty is more than 8 feet (2.4 m) tall.
- Lady Liberty's waist is 35 feet (10.7 m) around.

Movement

Winds of 50 miles (80.5 km) per hour can cause the statue to sway 3 inches (7.6 cm). The torch can sway 5 inches (12.7 cm).

Environmental Viewpoint

The environment can have a large effect on a statue. The Statue of Liberty is in an area that faces many types of weather and pollution. In the early 1980s, the statue was inspected to assess the damage that its environment had caused. The inspectors decided that the statue had to be restored.

Many factors caused the statue to need restoration. The humid air of the harbor had caused rust stains to appear on its exterior skin. It had caused corrosion on the interior iron frame. The torch and crown also had deteriorated due to **weathering**.

Bartholdi had selected copper for the exterior of the statue because of its resistance to corrosion. Over time, however, people had applied protective coatings to both the copper and the iron. When these coatings began to peel, the moist air was able to get into openings. This caused rust to appear. The worst corrosion occurred in areas where the two metals met. Galvanic corrosion caused the iron framework to swell and distort. This movement pulled many of the rivets out from the copper pieces that were holding them in place.

As a result, workers had to replace more than 30,000 copper rivets within the statue. Other parts, including 35,000 pounds of material for the framework, had to be replaced as well.

Even on a clear day, the Statue of Liberty is vulnerable to weather and pollution. The patina helps protect the statue from these elements.

In 1984, scaffolding was built around the Statue of Liberty, and the work to restore it finally began. Stainless steel was used to replace some of the iron bars, and steps were taken to reduce contact between the metals that made up the interior frame and the copper skin. It took two years to complete the restoration. The statue was reopened to the public on July 5, 1986. The entire project cost $62 million.

GALVANIC CORROSION

The main reason for the 1984 to 1986 restoration of the Statue of Liberty was galvanic corrosion. This type of corrosion occurs when two different types of metal, such as the copper used on the statue's exterior and the iron used on the interior frame, come into contact near electrical activity. In the case of the Statue of Liberty, the original designers had insulated the point of contact between the copper and iron with a cloth soaked in **shellac**. This protected the metals from corrosion for a while, but over time, the humid air of the harbor broke down the shellac. This left the metals without any protection from each other. The humidity caused an electrical, or galvanic, reaction to occur between the copper and iron. Corrosion was the result.

Construction Careers

Sculptor Frédéric Bartholdi planned all aspects of the Statue of Liberty before it was built. He picked a location, took measurements of the location, determined the materials the statue would be made of, and decided exactly how the statue would be built. To complete the construction of the Statue of Liberty, Bartholdi needed the help of many trade specialists, including metalworkers and laborers.

Sculptors

Sculptors are artists who design and build three-dimensional works of art. They may use a variety of techniques and materials to create their art. Sculpture can be created from many types of materials, such as wood, stone, clay, and metal. Some sculptors carve sculptures from these materials. Others, such as Bartholdi, may use molds to create shapes. Sculptors can use a variety of tools to create art. They may use their hands to mold materials into shape. Knives and **chisels** help chip pieces of rock. Mallets are used to pound softer materials. Sometimes, the materials are placed in a kiln. The heat sets the sculpture in a certain form.

Laborers

Laborers play a key role at any construction site. They get the materials into the hands of the people who need them. They do this by carrying the materials on their shoulders, carting them in wheelbarrows, and loading them onto trucks. Laborers help keep job sites clean. They know how to use tools, such as saws and hammers, and can operate a variety of construction equipment.

Metalworkers

Metalworkers were very important in the construction of the Statue of Liberty. They were responsible for putting all of the pieces in place. Metalworkers work with a set of blueprints to show them how the pieces of the structure fit together. They install the pieces by bolting or riveting them into place. Sometimes, metalworkers may weld pieces together.

This involves applying heat to the metal to **fuse** the pieces together. Metalworkers must have knowledge of different metals. They should also know the most effective methods and tools for working with metals.

Metalworkers should be in good physical condition and have strong mechanical skills.

Web Link:
To learn more about becoming a sculptor, visit www.xap.com/Career/careerdetail/career27-1013.04.html.

Notable Structures

There are many types of statues all around the world. Every statue has a different appearance, shape, and meaning. This is because they are considered works of art and represent the artist's viewpoint on a subject.

Christ the Redeemer

Built: 1931

Location: Corcovado Mountain, Rio de Janeiro, Brazil

Design: Heitor da Silva Costa and Paul Landowski

Description: This statue of Jesus Christ with outstretched arms is one of the **New Seven Wonders of the World.** The exterior is made of soapstone, and the inside is made of concrete. The statue stands as a symbol of **Christianity.**

Leshan Buddha

Built: started in 713 AD

Location: near Leshan, China

Design: Haitong

Description: The tallest stone Buddha in the world is also one of the world's oldest sculptures. It was carved out of the side of a cliff and has three rivers flowing at its feet. A Chinese monk named Haitong planned the building of this Buddha to calm the rough waters that made it difficult for boats to sail down the river.

Statues can be made of all types of materials, including stone and metal. They can be small or gigantic in size. Statues can represent a person, an animal, an object, or an idea.

Great Sphinx of Giza

Built: Around 2500 BC

Location: Giza Plateau, Egypt

Design: King Khafre

Description: The Great Sphinx is believed to have been built to guard King Khafre's temple. Made out of limestone, the Sphinx is a statue of a creature that is half-lion and half-human, with eagle wings. It remains a mystery as to what this statue represents.

Venus de Milo

Built: Around 190–100 BC

Location: The Louvre in Paris, France

Design: Alexandros of Antioch

Description: This marble statue is believed to represent Aphrodite, the Greek goddess of romantic love. It was found buried in ancient city ruins on the Aegean island of Milos. The statue was found in two pieces. These pieces were put together when the statue reached The Louvre. The arms were too damaged to be reattached.

Statues Around the World

Statues have been built and displayed all around the world. Each was built with its own purpose in mind. Some commemorate war heroes or are tributes to beauty.

ARCTIC
OCEAN

Structure: Nelson's Column
Location: London, England
Year: Between 1840 and 1843
Height: 18-foot (5.5-m) statue of Nelson stands on top of a 151-foot (46-m) column

NORTH
AMERICA

ATLANTIC
OCEAN

PACIFIC
OCEAN

Structure: The Thinker
Location: Paris, France
Year: 1902
Height: 6 feet (1.8 m)

SOUTH
AMERICA

Structure: The David
Location: Florence, Italy
Year: 1504
Height: 14 feet (4.3 m)

621 Miles
0   1,000 Kilometers

N
W · E
S

Others honor religious figures. All are meant to inspire those who view them. The following are just some of the best-known statues around the world.

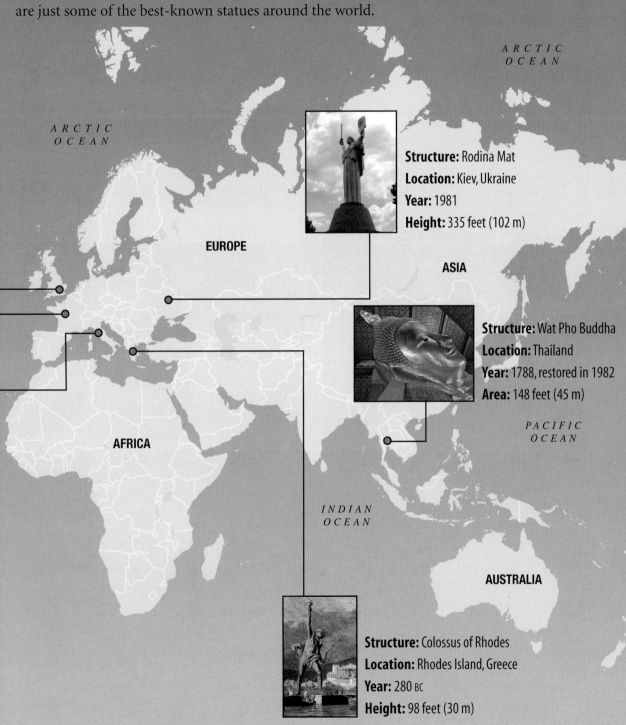

Structure: Rodina Mat
Location: Kiev, Ukraine
Year: 1981
Height: 335 feet (102 m)

Structure: Wat Pho Buddha
Location: Thailand
Year: 1788, restored in 1982
Area: 148 feet (45 m)

Structure: Colossus of Rhodes
Location: Rhodes Island, Greece
Year: 280 BC
Height: 98 feet (30 m)

Quiz

Q What does the Statue of Liberty symbolize?

A The statue symbolizes liberty and the escape from oppression.

Q Who designed the Statue of Liberty?

A Frédéric Auguste Bartholdi designed the statue.

Q What two metals make up most of the statue?

A The statue is made up mainly of copper and iron. The copper is the outside skin, and the iron is the interior framework.

Q Why did the Statue of Liberty need to be restored in 1984?

A The statue needed to be restored due to damage caused by weathering and corrosion.

Testing Corrosion

Copper and iron were used to build the Statue of Liberty because they are very durable metals. Try this experiment to see which metal corrodes the fastest. You will need to observe the metals over a 10-day period and make notes every day.

Materials
- two pieces silver wire
- two pieces copper wire
- two pieces iron wire
- six clear drinking glasses
- six pencils
- salt
- distilled water
- a sheet of paper

Instructions
1. Cut the paper to make six labels. Mark each of the labels as follows: a) water and silver; b) salt water and silver; c) water and copper; d) salt water and copper; e) water and steel; f) salt water and steel.

2. Set the glasses in a row on a counter, and place one label in front of each glass.

3. Fill three of the glasses with distilled water, and place with the appropriate label.

4. Mix 3 cups of water with 2 tablespoons of salt until the salt is dissolved.

5. Fill the remaining three cups with the salt water.

6. Wrap one end of each piece of wire around a pencil, leaving enough wire to touch the bottom of the glass.

7. Balance the pencil on the top of each marked glass, and hang the wire into the water and salt water.

8. Check on the wires every day for the next 10 days. Look for changes such as rust. Observe and compare if the wire corroded more in the distilled water or salt water. Watch for where the metal rusts—if it is only on one part of the wire or all over.

Further Research

You can find out more about the Statue of Liberty and its construction, as well as other statues of the world, at your local library or on the Internet.

Websites

For more information on the Statue of Liberty, visit
www.nps.gov/stli

Find out more about the construction of the Statue of Liberty at
www.statueliberty.net

Learn more about statues around the world at
www.garden-fountains.com/famous-statues/
statues-main-page.htm

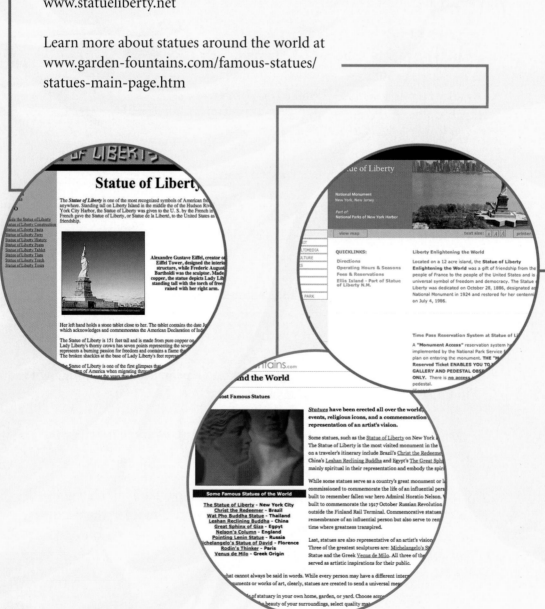

Glossary

architect: a person who designs buildings

chisels: hand tools consisting of a flat steel blade with a handle

Christianity: a religion that believes in and follows the teachings of Jesus Christ

democracy: a form of government in which the public directs policy through its representatives

foundation: the part of a building that helps support its weight

fuse: unite by melting

landmarks: certain objects on Earth that can be used to mark a piece of land

monarch: a king or queen

New Seven Wonders of the World: the seven structures considered by scholars to be the most wondrous of the modern world

oppression: a feeling of being weighed down within a person's mind or body

perpendicular: at right angles

republics: states in which the supreme power is held by the people and not by a king or queen

restore: the act of renewing and reviving

shellac: a type of varnish, or protective coating

UNESCO World Heritage Site: a site designated by the United Nations to be of great cultural worth to the world and in need of protection

weathering: a chemical process that makes rocks decompose

Index